# SUPERBOATS

## IAN GRAHAM

Heinemann
LIBRARY

# H www.heinemann.co.uk/library

Visit our website to find out more information about **Heinemann Library** books.

To order:
- ☎ Phone 44 (0) 1865 888066
- 🖹 Send a fax to 44 (0) 1865 314091
- 🖥 Visit the Heinemann Bookshop at www.heinemann.co.uk/library to browse our catalogue and order online.

First published in Great Britain by Heinemann Library, Halley Court, Jordan Hill, Oxford, OX2 8EJ, part of Harcourt Education.
Heinemann is a registered trademark of Harcourt Education Ltd.

Editorial: Andrew Farrow and Dan Nunn
Design: Jo Hinton-Malivoire and Tinstar Design Limited (www.tinstar.co.uk)
Illustrations: Geoff Ward
Picture Research: Rebecca Sodergren and Bob Battersby
Production: Viv Hichens

Originated by Dot Gradations Ltd
Printed and bound in China by South China Printing Company

ISBN 0 431 16565 3 (hardback)
07 06 05 04 03
10 9 8 7 6 5 4 3 2 1

ISBN 0 431 16572 6 (paperback)
08 07 06 05 04
10 9 8 7 6 5 4 3 2 1

**British Library Cataloguing in Publication Data**
Graham, Ian, 1953 –
    Superboats. – (Designed for Success)
    1. Boats and boating – Juvenile literature
    I. Title
    623.8'2
A full catalogue record for this book is available from the British Library.

**Acknowledgements**
The publishers would like to thank the following for permission to reproduce photographs: Alvey & Towers pp. **5** (bottom), **7** (top), **11** (top), **11** (bottom), **15** (top), **25** (bottom); Alvey & Towers/Peter Wilson p. **4**; Australian National Maritime Museum p. **27** (bottom); Corbis pp. **18**, **19** (top), **19** (bottom), **21** (bottom); Kos Picture Source/G-J Norman p. **8**; Kos Picture Source/Gilles Martin-Raget p. **23** (top); Miss Freei p. **27** (top); Nautica International p. **21**; PA Photos pp. **16** (large picture), **28**; PA Photos/Ben Curtis p. **26**; PA Photos/Chris Ison p. **9** (bottom); PA Photos/EPA pp. **9** (top), **25** (top); Princess International p. **5** (top); R. D. Battersby/Tografox pp. **11** (middle), **12**, **13** (top), **13** (bottom left), **13** (bottom right), **15** (bottom), **24**; Rick Tomlinson Photography p. **25** (middle); Skiers Choice p. **6**; Steven Piantieri p. **16** (inset); Sunseeker pp. **10**, **14**; TRH Pictures/Sealine p. **23** (bottom); TRH/Racal Decca p. **7** (bottom); TRH/US Navy p. **17** (bottom); US Library of Congress p. **29**.

Cover photograph reproduced with permission of Corbis.

Every effort has been made to contact copyright holders of any material reproduced in this book. Any omissions will be rectified in subsequent printings if notice is given to the publishers.

# CONTENTS

Any words appearing in the text in bold, **like this**, are explained in the Glossary.

# HIGH-PERFORMANCE BOATS

High-performance boats are the fastest, most powerful and most luxurious of powerboats. They are enjoyed and raced on the world's rivers, lakes and seas. They range from **personal watercraft** to luxurious motor yachts, and from tiny one-person **hydroplanes** to roaring 2000-**horsepower** offshore racing powerboats. They can have one, two or even three hulls.

The hull is the part of a boat that sits in the water. Many high-performance boats have hulls called **planing hulls**. These are designed to ride on top of the water instead of trying to push their way through it. Hydrofoil boats ride on underwater **planes** that lift their hulls above the surface of the water altogether.

## OFFSHORE RACERS

Racing powerboats, like this catamaran, can race around an offshore course at average speeds of more than 110 **knots** (200 kmph/125 mph). At top speed they carve up the surf and leap from wave to wave. To keep up this sort of performance for a whole race, these racing boats have to be immensely powerful and strong.

## ROYALTY AFLOAT

The Princess V65 is a modern luxury motor yacht. The 20-metre boat is powered by twin high-speed **diesel engines**. These two 1300-horsepower units give it a top speed of 41 knots, or about 76 kmph (47 mph). Its hull is designed to combine fast and efficient **propulsion** with a stable, comfortable ride. The yacht's sumptuous interior includes a home entertainment centre with television, DVD, VCR, hi-fi and surround sound. And it has built-in twin garages for small boats or personal watercraft!

## DESIGN FACTORS

All of these boats have to be designed. They have to be the right shape and weight. They have to be big enough, but not too big. Their engines have to be the right size and power. Cost is an important factor in their design. They have to be affordable, and they have to look good too. A boat's designer has to consider all of these matters.

### Princess V65 sports cruiser

Length: 20.3 metres

Width: 5.1 metres

Engine: 2 x 22-litre V12s

Propulsion: propeller

Top speed: 41 knots (76 kmph/47 mph)

## COME FLY WITH ME!

Passengers can skim over the tops of the waves in hydrofoils. When a hydrofoil takes off, it isn't slowed down or buffeted by surface waves any more. This gives its passengers a much faster and smoother journey. When passenger hydrofoils became popular in the 1950s, they were so much faster than existing boats that they slashed some journey-times by three-quarters.

# SPORT AND LEISURE BOATS

Sport and leisure boats are designed for the activity they will be used for. For example, this might be luxury cruising or it might be towing water-skiers. The form of the boat (its shape) follows from its function (what it's used for).

Sport and leisure boats are mostly **monohulls**. The single hull has lots of room inside for seating, engines and, in larger boats, cabins. The bow (front) of the hull is V-shaped to cut through the water. A deep V-hull is more comfortable than a broad, shallow V-hull, because the boat rolls from side to side less. However, a broader V-hull has more space inside. The designer has to balance these factors.

## WAKE UP!

All boats create a **wake** behind them – a trail of churned-up water. Sports boats are now designed to produce the right shape of wake for different water-sports! For example, **wake-boarders** like a higher wake than water-skiers for doing tricks. Some boats are designed to let the driver change the shape of the wake.

Pumping water into **ballast** tanks raises or lowers the bow and changes the wake's shape. The Supra Launch (shown here) uses a different system. It has an adjustable wake board at the stern. Raising or lowering the board changes the shape of the wake.

### Supra Launch sports boat

Length: 6.4 metres

Width: 2.5 metres

Engine: 5.7-litre petrol

Propulsion: propeller

Top speed: 39 knots (72 kmph/45 mph)

## GPS MARKS THE SPOT

For centuries, sailors steered by the Sun and stars or by measuring how fast they travelled for a certain time in a particular direction. However, these methods were not very accurate. Then the US government developed a Global Positioning System (GPS) so that its military forces could find their precise location. Now everyone can use it. A GPS receiver picks up radio signals from satellites orbiting the Earth. It works out how far away the satellites are and from this calculates its exact position.

## SEEING WITH RADIO

Most large sea-going powerboats are equipped with radar. Radar can 'see' at night and in fog. It sends out bursts of radio waves in all directions and picks up any reflections that bounce back off objects such as other boats. The reflections are shown on a screen.

## LOOK OUT!

A clear view around a boat is vital to avoid accidents. A speedboat driver can sit down in the hull and still have a good view because the boat is so small and sits so low in the water. Larger motor-yachts need a raised **cockpit** or bridge above their cabins to let the driver see all round the boat.

# RACING POWERBOATS

Racing boats are designed differently from leisure boats. Speed and strength are more important than comfort and space for cabins, sun-decks and baggage storage.

If the boat is to be a **monohull**, a long, narrow V-shaped **planing hull** works well. The V-shaped bow (front) cuts through the waves easily and the planing hull is fast over the water. Its long, narrow shape also reduces **air resistance**. The stern (rear) of the boat houses a powerful petrol or **diesel engine**.

Most big racing boats today are **catamarans** – they have two hulls side-by-side. Catamarans are popular because their two ultra-slim hulls slip through the water faster than one big hull. The wide shape of the boat also makes it roll from side to side less than a monohull. Power is supplied by engines in each hull. A high-power 'cat' like the *Spirit of Norway* can reach more than 130 **knots** (240 kmph/150 mph) when racing at full-speed in calm water.

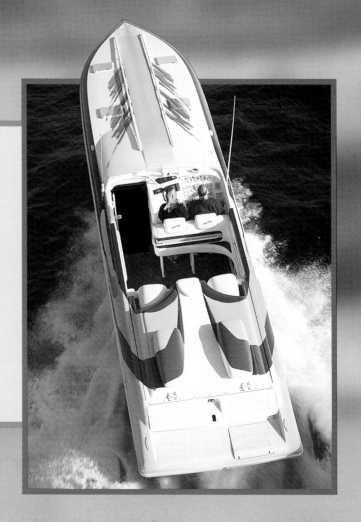

## CIGARETTE RACING

The longest, slimmest and fastest monohull racing boats are also known as 'cigarette boats' in the USA. They are named after *Cigarette*, one of the first successful ocean racing boats. The US Cigarette Racing Team is one of the most successful teams in powerboat racing. Its boats have won a host of national and international powerboat championships since the 1960s.

## RACING IN A BUBBLE

So much of a racing powerboat sits above the water that its **performance** in air is as important as its performance in water. To cut down air resistance, the fastest racing boats have enclosed **cockpits**. The crew sit under a **streamlined**, bubble-shaped canopy. Some of the big racing cats have a cockpit in each hull.

### Spirit of Norway racing cat

Length: 14.2 metres

Width: 3.95 metres

Engine: 2 x 8.2-litre V12s

Propulsion: propeller

Top speed: 130+ knots (240+ kmph/150+ mph)

The racing catamaran *Spirit of Norway* speeds across the wave-tops, driven by two powerful diesel engines and propellers.

## STEPPING OUT

The bottom of a racing hull is not perfectly smooth. It looks as if it has been cut from side to side and the front section sits a little lower than the rear section. It's called a **stepped hull**. As the boat accelerates, it rises up onto the lowest part of the hull. This reduces **drag**, because less of the hull has to push through the water. Air is sucked underneath the hull along channels at each side of the step. The mixture of air and water under the boat reduces drag even more. It works like oil lubricating the moving parts of an engine, and lets the boat go much faster.

The stepped hull is clearly visible on boat C-54 – it looks as if someone has cut slices into the boat!

# SUNSEEKER XS2000
## DESIGN FLAIR

The Sunseeker XS2000 is a world-class high-performance powerboat. It is designed to be equally at home as a luxury sports boat or a serious racing boat. Its slim, elegant hull is 11.85 metres long and **stepped** underneath. It is designed to skim effortlessly over the water's surface at high speed. Its clean lines are designed to cut **drag** and **air resistance** to a minimum. A shallow windshield in front of the **cockpit** deflects air up and over the crew. The cockpit itself is designed for racing, with separate seats for the **helmsman** and the co-pilot.

Power for the XS2000 is supplied by twin **diesel** 420-**horsepower** engines driving two 'surface-piercing' propellers. By using a combination of materials carefully chosen for strength and lightness, the boat's weight has been kept down to 5000 kilograms. Keeping weight down is important, because a lighter boat can accelerate faster and reach higher speeds.

The sleek, slender Sunseeker XS2000 is designed to be one of the world's fastest powerboats.

## SNORKELLING

The XS2000's special **propellers** are called surface-piercing propellers because they are designed to work best with only their bottom half under water. However, when the boat sets off, the propellers are completely submerged. To ensure that they work at their best, a pipe supplies the top half of each propeller with air from the surface. The pipes, called snorkels, enable the propellers to spin more freely. They come up to speed faster while the boat accelerates to its planing speed.

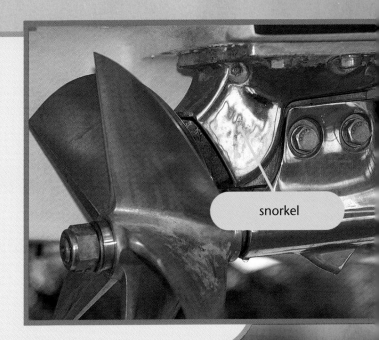

snorkel

## OPEN SESAME!

At the press of a switch, a motorized cover in front of the cockpit slides forward to reveal an extra seating area. Hatches in this area open up to give access to a cabin inside the hull. Closing up the cover restores the deck's **streamlined** shape.

## ANTI-STUFF NOSE

Ideally, a designer would like a boat to sit absolutely level as it speeds across flat, calm water. Unfortunately, the sea is rarely flat and calm. Therefore the boat is certain to roll and pitch as it hits waves and troughs in the water. In rough water, the XS2000's nose might actually pitch down low enough to plough under the surface. Its nose has two 18-centimetre wings, called anti-stuff planes, designed to lift the nose and get it out of the water again fast.

anti-stuff plane

# SUNSEEKER XS2000
## LIGHTNESS IN STRENGTH

The Sunseeker XS2000 is built from new materials, called composites, which are chosen for their strength and lightness. The main part of the hull is made from **glass reinforced plastic** (**GRP**). It's called a composite because it's made from at least two different materials – in this case, a plastic called epoxy and **glass fibre**. The composite made from them is stronger than either of the separate materials.

GRP is an ideal material for making boats because it can be moulded into almost any shape. Traditional wooden hulls can rot if they are not painted or varnished to stop water soaking into them. GRP does not rot or need as much maintenance as wood. The parts of the hull that have to be the strongest are made from Kevlar, a composite material made from plastic fibres instead of glass fibres.

## MAKING GLASS HULLS

Construction of a GRP hull begins with a mould that looks like the boat's hull turned inside out.
- First, the mould is painted with something called a releasing agent so that the hull will not stick to it.
- Next a thick gel coat is painted onto the mould. This forms the smooth outer surface of the hull.
- Mats of hair-thin strands of glass are laid on top of the gel and soaked with liquid **epoxy resin**.
- When the resin sets hard, the hull is pulled out of the mould.

## JELLY MOULDS

A GRP hull or deck on its own is almost as flimsy as a jelly. So, designers add parts to strengthen the boat so that it holds its shape. The strengthening parts that run the length of the boat are called stringers. Those that run across the hull are called bulkheads. Some of these strengthening parts are made from GRP with wood inside. Balsa wood was chosen for the filling because of its incredible lightness. Balsa wood on its own is very fragile. However, parts made from these two materials sandwiched together have the best properties of both of them — they are as tough as the GRP and as light as the balsa wood.

A finished XS2000 is launched for trials on the water.

## WEIGHT TAMING

The XS2000's twin diesel engines are the heaviest parts of the boat. They have to be positioned in exactly the right place. Too far forward and the boat's bow (front) would sit too low. Too far back and the bow would sit too high. They also have to be mounted securely so that they cannot move. They are bolted to metal plates moulded into the hull.

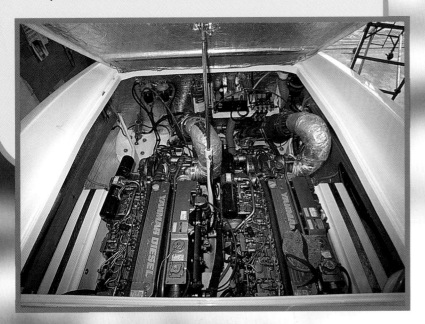

# SUNSEEKER XS2000
## PURE PERFORMANCE

The Sunseeker XS2000 is the world's fastest production powerboat. It is fast enough to fly across metre-high waves at 80 **knots** (150 kmph), but can still be manoeuvred around a dock at walking pace.

One reason for such a versatile **performance** is the use of a two-speed **transmission**. This means there are two gears to choose from, rather like driving a car. This enables the engine to drive the propellers over two different speed ranges. The boat sets off in low gear. Pushing the **throttle** control forwards makes it accelerate sharply. The hull quickly rises up into the planing position. At about 40 knots (75 kmph), the transmission shifts into high gear and the boat accelerates to its top speed. On the straight, the boat rises high, up on its hull and planes over the water. Throw the **helm** over and the boat responds instantly, heeling over into a tight turn. A pure racing version of the boat, the XSR2000, is also available, with an even more spectacular performance.

## WORLD-BEATER

On 24 July 2001 a standard XS2000, like the one on the right, set four world records and two British records.

- It became the fastest boat over 6, 12, 18 and 24 hours.
- In 24 hours circling the Isle of Wight, off the south coast of England, it covered a distance of 1770 kilometres at an average speed of 46 knots (85 kmph).
- It also set new British records for the fastest five-lap and ten-lap times around the Isle of Wight.

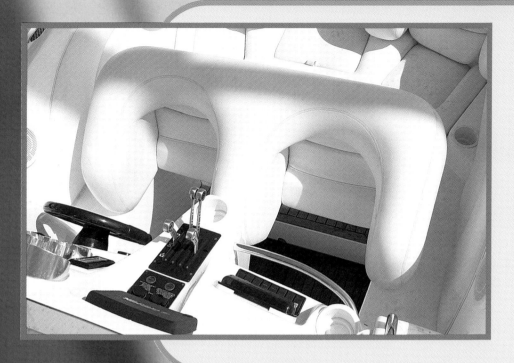

## ALL STAND!

The XS2000 is built to perform like a racing powerboat. Its cockpit is laid out for racing. The crew drive the boat standing up, strapped into supports called bolsters. A bench seat behind them can hold three more people. The engine throttle and gear controls are mounted, racing style, between the two bolsters so that either driver can operate them.

### Sunseeker XS2000

Length: 11.85 metres

Width: 2.3 metres

Engine: twin 420-hp inboard diesels

Propulsion: propeller

Top speed: 80 knots (150 kmph/93 mph)

## DONE TO A TURN

The XS2000 can turn amazingly sharply. It is steered by turning a **rudder** behind each propeller. The rudder is a panel that can swivel to one side, so that it lies at an angle to the water rushing past the boat. The water hits the rudder and pushes the stern (rear) of the boat to one side, swinging the front end round to point in a new direction.

# ENGINE POWER

Most boats are powered by the same sort of petrol and **diesel** piston engines that power cars. The most exotic boats are propelled by jet engines.

A boat's engine may be **outboard** (hung on the outside) or **inboard** (housed inside the hull). This choice affects the design of the hull and the way the boat is steered.

- Boats with outboard engines are steered by turning the whole engine and **propeller**. Bigger engines are housed inside the hull and the boat is usually steered by turning a **rudder**.
- Some powerboats use a system called a stern-drive, or out-drive. This enables a boat with an inboard engine to steer by swivelling the propeller.
- A few large, fast boats use **water-jet engines**. They pump water out of the boat's stern at high speed.
- A handful of boats use jet engines. The engine can propel the boat by jet **thrust**, like a jet aeroplane, or by spinning a shaft that drives a propeller or water-jet.

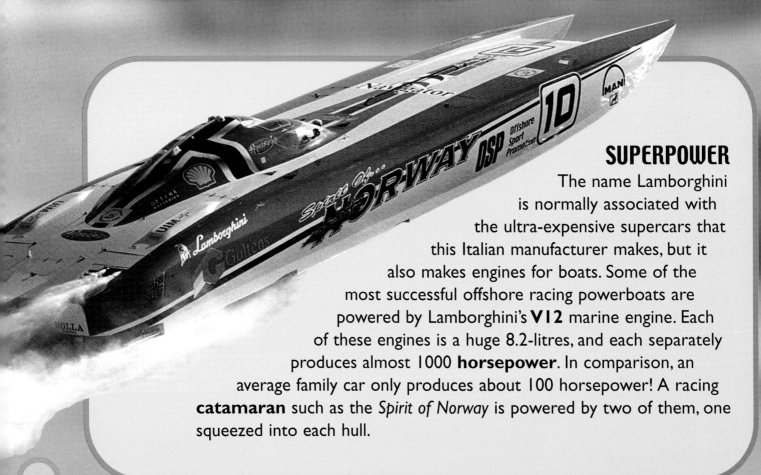

## SUPERPOWER

The name Lamborghini is normally associated with the ultra-expensive supercars that this Italian manufacturer makes, but it also makes engines for boats. Some of the most successful offshore racing powerboats are powered by Lamborghini's **V12** marine engine. Each of these engines is a huge 8.2-litres, and each separately produces almost 1000 **horsepower**. In comparison, an average family car only produces about 100 horsepower! A racing **catamaran** such as the *Spirit of Norway* is powered by two of them, one squeezed into each hull.

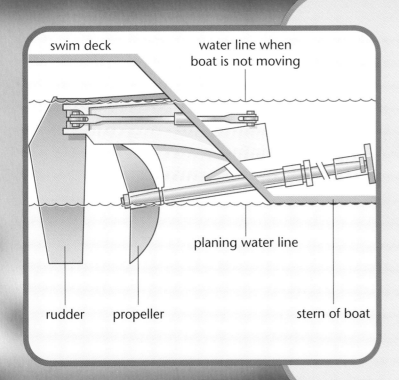

swim deck

water line when boat is not moving

planing water line

rudder

propeller

stern of boat

## PUSHY BLADES

A propeller works by producing a force that pushes a boat through the water. Its blades are set at an angle so that when the propeller spins, they push backwards against the water. Most boat propellers are completely submerged, but high-performance boats often use propellers that run with half the propeller blades out of the water at any given time. They're called surface-piercing propellers. They are larger and spin more slowly than submerged propellers. Surprisingly, this makes them more efficient than smaller, faster, submerged propellers.

## FLY NAVY

A **hydrofoil** is a boat that uses underwater wings to lift its hull out of the water. The US Navy gunboat *Tucumcari* was the first large hydrofoil to be powered by a water-jet engine instead of propellers. It was launched in 1967.

TUCUMCARI

The 22-metre long, 58-tonne *Tucumcari* could travel at nearly 50 knots (90 kmph) in all weathers.

# HYDROPLANES

**Hydroplanes** are the Grand Prix racers of the boating world. These small, light boats skim across the water's surface incredibly fast. Hydroplanes are designed to ride on top of the water, not through it. As a hydroplane speeds up, air rushes into a tunnel under the boat. It is the pressure of this trapped air that pushes the boat upwards. Eventually, the boat rises up so high that it touches the water at only three points – two floats, called sponsons, at the front and the **propeller** at the back. For this reason, these boats are also called three-point hydroplanes, or prop-riders.

Older **inboard** hydroplanes had their engine at the front with the driver sitting behind. Modern inboard hydroplanes, called cabovers, are designed the opposite way round. The engine is at the back and the driver sits at the front. The cabover design is faster because the engine is mounted lower down. This lets the boat turn faster without tipping over.

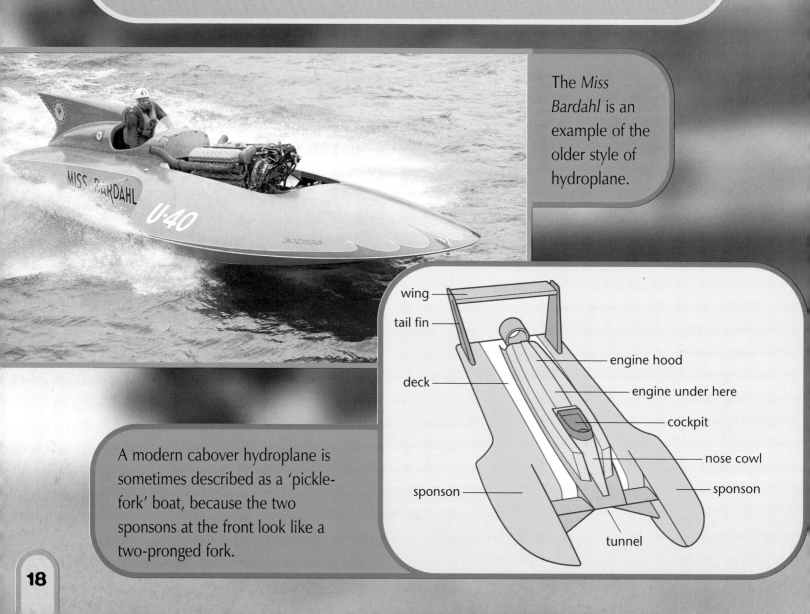

The *Miss Bardahl* is an example of the older style of hydroplane.

MISS BARDAHL
U-40
3OZ1558

A modern cabover hydroplane is sometimes described as a 'pickle-fork' boat, because the two sponsons at the front look like a two-pronged fork.

wing
tail fin
deck
engine hood
engine under here
cockpit
nose cowl
sponson
sponson
tunnel

## WAVE DANCER

The U-1 cabover hydroplane dances across the water, barely touching the surface. The huge opening above the cockpit sucks air into an Avco Lycoming T-55 L-7 **gas turbine engine** that sits behind the driver. The engine drives a 40-centimetre, three-blade propeller. The driver is protected from accidents by a bullet-proof canopy from an F-16 fighter plane!

### U-1 cabover hydroplane

Length: 9.0 metres

Width: 4.4 metres

Engine: gas turbine

Propulsion: propeller

Top speed: 135 knots (250 kmph/155 mph)

## SKID TURNS

Hydroplanes have a small fin, called a skid fin. It is there to help the boat turn. Other vehicles, such as bicycles and cars, are able to turn by pushing against the ground. However, a hydroplane designed to sit on top of the water can't push against it when the driver tries to turn. The skid fin, dipping under the surface, solves this problem.

# FLOATING ON AIR

Rescue services and security forces use boats called RIBs (Rigid Inflatable Boats), because they are small, fast and light. RIBs range from tiny rowing boat-sized models for use on lakes and rivers to bigger offshore and ocean-going boats. The same design features make them very good for leisure, sport and racing.

RIBs have a rigid hull with an inflated tube, or collar, around the top to give them **buoyancy**. Being **inflatable**, they are extremely light, easy to handle and virtually unsinkable.

- The air-filled collar is divided into a series of watertight compartments. If one is pierced, the others stay inflated and keep the boat afloat.
- The RIB's hull is V-shaped at the bow (front) and flatter at the stern (rear), forming a **planing** surface that rides on top of the water.
- The hull is usually made from **glass reinforced plastic** (**GRP**).
- The collar is made from a sandwich of materials that are tough, flexible and airtight.

## RUBBER SANDWICHES

RIB collars are made from a sandwich of at least three different materials. A tough tube of polyester fabric is lined with a rubber-like material, such as neoprene. The polyester gives the tube strength so that it doesn't tear apart. The lining material makes it airtight. On the outside, the polyester is covered with a layer of tough material such as PVC. This covering provides a smooth outer surface and protects the collar from oil, petrol and ultra-violet rays in sunlight.

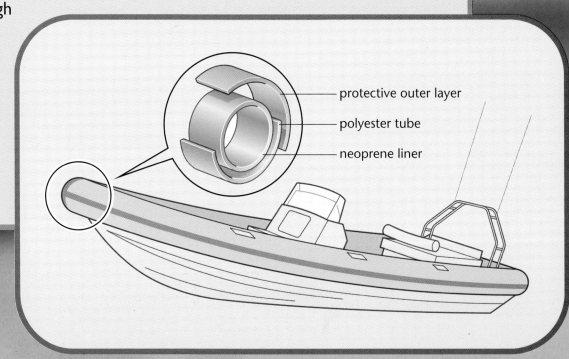

protective outer layer

polyester tube

neoprene liner

## CAT RIBS

Most RIBs are **monohulls**, but they can be made in any shape. **Catamaran** RIBs are very popular because of the extra stability their twin-hull design gives them. The Nautica RIB 20 is a catamaran RIB with a ramp in the bow. It can use the ramp as a diving platform at sea, or lower it on a beach to unload people or cargo.

## SUPER RIB

RIBs have become so popular that there are now luxury models and racing versions. The *Hot Lemon II* shown here is a high-performance RIB. Its 'Hot Lemon' name was inspired by its mainly yellow colour. Its successors, *Hot Lemon III* and *Hot Lemon IV*, have been equally successful. They set Round Britain records in 2001 and 2002 respectively. *Hot Lemon III* is an 8.75-metre RIB weighing 3600 kg while *Hot Lemon IV* is a 10-metre RIB of the same design.

### Hot Lemon III

Length: 8.75 metres

Width: 2.62 metres

Engine: 300 hp diesel inboard engine

Propulsion: propeller

Top speed: 42 knots (80 kmph/50 mph)

# FLYING BOATS

Hydrofoils are designed to go faster than other boats by 'flying' above the water. They use underwater wings to lift their hull out of the water altogether.

When a hydrofoil sits at rest, it looks much the same as any other boat. As it sets off and speeds up, something strange happens. The hull rises up and eventually the boat takes off and flies above the water. Its weight is supported by wings, called **foils**, which are designed to 'fly' through water. They are tiny compared to aircraft wings, because water is thicker than air. A small foil slowly cutting through water can produce as much **lift** as a big wing slicing much faster through the air. Lifting the hull out of the water cuts the **drag** it normally produces and lets the boat travel faster while also burning less fuel. Underwater foils are not affected by waves on the surface, so hydrofoils can sail smoothly in bad weather.

## 'V' FOR HYDROFOIL

Most passenger hydrofoils are fitted with V-shaped foils. They automatically keep the boat at the right height. If the boat loses height as it flies along, more of the V-foils sink under the water. There, they produce more lift and so the boat rises again. If it rises too high, more of the V-foils come up out of the water. They produce less lift and the boat settles down lower again.

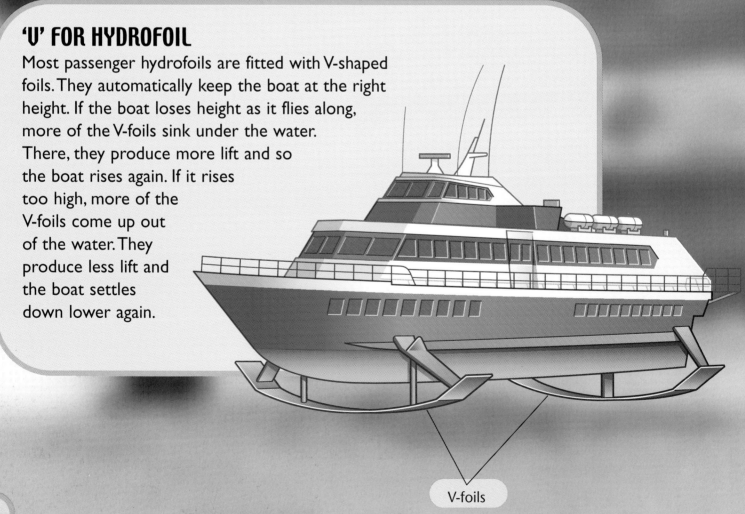

V-foils

## FLYING SAIL-BOATS

Sailing boats can fly too. *Hydroptere* is a hydrofoil sailboat. It has three foils – one at each side of its hull and a third in the shape of an upside-down 'T' at its stern. The T-foil also acts as a **rudder**. The 21-metre long, 4900-kilogram boat reached a top speed of 41 **knots** (76 kmph) in sea trials.

## JET BOATS

The Boeing Jetfoil is a **water-jet**-powered hydrofoil. As it flies along, it measures its height above the water by bouncing **ultrasonic** sound waves off the water and timing how long they take to come back. Information from this and other instruments controls the position of the flaps in its underwater foils. Swivelling the flaps controls the boat's height.

### Boeing 929-100 Jetfoil

Length: 27.4 metres
Width: 9.1 metres
Engine: 2 x jet engines
Propulsion: water-jets
Top speed: 46 knots (85 kmph/53 mph)

# SAFETY FIRST

Designers and boat-builders make their boats as safe as possible, but accidents can still happen. So, boats of all sizes carry extra safety equipment designed to protect the crew and passengers.

Safety equipment used on water is designed to work in two different ways. First, it ensures that people stay afloat and then, if necessary, it summons help. If any crew or passengers fall in the water, life jackets and, on larger boats, life rafts keep them afloat. If help is needed, radio, lights and flares attract attention. Safety is particularly important in racing, where things can go spectacularly wrong in the blink of an eye. Racing boat crews are often cocooned inside a 'survival cell' similar to the **cockpit** of a Formula 1 motor-racing car – and they wear similar safety clothing, too.

## STAYING AFLOAT

The most important piece of safety equipment carried at sea is the life jacket. There are two types. Both are designed to keep someone afloat if he or she falls into water.

- The first type is filled with foam plastic. Air bubbles in the foam make them very **buoyant**. However, the foam also makes them quite bulky and cumbersome.
- The second type (pictured below) is lighter and thinner. When it is needed, it is filled up with gas from a small built-in cylinder. These **inflatable** jackets are either operated by the wearer or they may be triggered automatically when they fall into water.

A high-**performance** boat can turn over in a fraction of a second if it hits a wave or another boat's **wake** at an awkward angle.

This picture shows a flare being used by a man overboard.

## FLARING UP

If a boat has no radio or the radio isn't working, the crew need another way of signalling that they need help. They can summon help and show where they are by using flares. A flare is designed to burn slowly, like a large match, and produce lots of light or smoke or both. Parachute flares are fired up into the sky and descend slowly under a mini-parachute.

## STAYING ALIVE

Racing boat crews wear a life jacket and a crash helmet. An intercom built into each helmet lets the crew members talk to each other. Crew members thrown overboard may be unconscious, so their life jackets are designed to turn them over on to their backs to keep their faces out of the water.

# RECORD-SETTERS

The boats that set speed records are extremely high-**performance** boats. They combine the most powerful engines with the sleekest hulls to reach the highest speeds.

The designers of high-performance boats sometimes use parts designed for other fast vehicles. Jet engines developed for use in helicopters and fighters are often put to use in boats specially designed to break records. Helicopter engines are designed to spin a rotor, so they can be easily modified to spin a boat's **propeller** instead. Fighter engines are designed to propel a plane by jet **thrust**, and they're used in the same way in record-breaking boats. The boat is pushed along by the jet of fiery hot gas produced by the engine. The shape of the boat is very important too. Record-breakers often use the shape that is most successful in racing – the **hydroplane**.

## ROUND-THE-WORLD ADVENTURE

In 1998, the dramatic design of the powerboat *Cable & Wireless Adventurer* enabled it to sail around the world faster than any other boat had done before. It was designed as a type of **monohull** called a very slender vessel (VSV). A VSV is very fast, but its long, slim hull rolls a lot in heavy seas. To stop this, *Adventurer* has two smaller **outrigger** floats attached to the main hull. The 35-metre, 50-tonne boat circled the globe in 75 days – 8 days faster than the previous record-holder, the US nuclear submarine *Triton*.

## FAST LADY

On 15 June 2000 a hydroplane called *Miss Freei* made history, with Russ Wicks at the wheel. It skimmed across the surface of Lake Washington in the USA at an average speed of 179 **knots** or 330 kmph. It was the highest speed that any propeller-driven boat had ever reached. *Miss Freei*'s propeller is driven by a **gas turbine engine** that normally powers a Chinook military helicopter!

## STAR PERFORMER

On 8 October 1978 Ken Warby became the fastest person ever to travel on water. He set a record speed of 276 knots or 511 kmph in his boat *Spirit of Australia* on Blowering Dam Lake in Australia. Warby built the boat himself. He chose a Westinghouse J34 jet engine to provide the enormous thrust needed to set the record.

### *Miss Freei* hydroplane

Length: 9.1 metres

Width: 4.4 metres

Engine: Lycoming L7C gas turbine

Propulsion: propeller

Top speed: 191 knots (355 kmph/220 mph)

# DATA FILES

Leisure and racing powerboats vary a great deal in their size, means of **propulsion** and **performance**. Here are data for a range of these boats.

| Boat | Length (metres) | Width (metres) | Propulsion | Top speed (knots / kmph) |
|---|---|---|---|---|
| Boeing 929-100 Jetfoil | 27.40 | 9.10 | Water-jet | 46 / 85 |
| *Cable & Wireless Adventurer* | 35.00 | 14.10 | Propeller | 27 / 50 |
| Cigarette *Top Gun* powerboat | 11.40 | 2.40 | Propeller | 78 / 145 |
| *Hot Lemon III* RIB | 8.75 | 2.62 | Propeller | 42 / 80 |
| *Hydroptere* hydrofoil yacht | 21.00 | 18.30 | Sail | 41 / 76 |
| *Miss Freei* hydroplane | 9.10 | 4.40 | Propeller | 191 / 355 |
| Princess V65 sports cruiser | 20.30 | 5.10 | Jet thrust | 41 / 76 |
| *Spirit of Australia* hydroplane | 8.20 | 2.40 | Propeller | 276 / 511 |
| *Spirit of Norway* racing catamaran | 14.20 | 3.95 | Propeller | 130+ / 240+ |
| Sunseeker XS2000 | 11.85 | 2.30 | Propeller | 80 / 150 |
| Supra Launch sports boat | 6.40 | 2.50 | Propeller | 39 / 72 |

## JET BOAT

The first boat powered by jet **thrust** to set an outright world water speed record was the *Bluebird K7* **hydroplane** driven by Donald Campbell. Between 1955 and 1964, Campbell set seven world water speed records in the boat and raised the record from 155 knots or 287 kmph to 241 knots or 445 kmph. In 1964, he also held the land speed record, making him the only person ever to hold both the land and water speed records at the same time.

# FURTHER READING AND RESEARCH

## BOOKS

*Boats (Built for Speed)*, by Ian Graham, Belitha Press, 1997
*Boats (Speedy Machines)*, by Vic Parker, Belitha Press, 1999
*The Amazing Book of Paper Boats*, by Jeremy Roberts, Chronicle Books, 2001
*The High-Speed Boats*, by S. Bornhoft, Franklin Watts, 1999

## WEBSITES

http://www.boatsafe.com/kids
An excellent website that answers lots of questions about boats.

http://www.anzsbeg.org.au/kids.html
The website of the Australia and New Zealand Safe Boating Education
Group, with information and games about boats.

http://boatingsidekicks.com/kidsknow/knowmain.htm
A website full of lots of boating know-how from the National Safe Boating
Council.

http://www.eagle.ca/~matink/themes/Transport/water.html
An educational website full of information and links about all sorts of boats
and water transport.

## FIRST FOILER

The first **hydrofoil** boat (pictured right) was built in 1905 by its inventor, Enrico Forlanini. The **foils** were stacked up above each other like the rungs of a ladder. Alexander Graham Bell, the inventor of the telephone, bought a licence from Forlanini to build his hydrofoils in the USA.

# GLOSSARY

**air resistance** the force of air pushing against anything that tries to move through it

**ballast** a heavy substance placed in the bottom of a boat to make it more stable. Water can be used as ballast.

**buoyant/buoyancy** the ability to float – if something is buoyant, it floats

**catamaran** type of boat with two hulls side by side instead of one – catamarans are sometimes called 'cats'

**cockpit** the part of a sports or racing boat where the crew sits

**diesel engine** type of engine used by larger boats because of its power and reliability

**drag** a force that slows a boat down as it moves through water

**epoxy resin** a liquid chemical that sets hard, which is used in boat-building

**foil** short for hydrofoil, a wing-shaped part of a hydrofoil boat. Underwater foils cut through the water and create a force that lifts the boat's hull out of the water.

**gas turbine engine** another name for a jet engine

**glass fibre** a material made from mats of hair-thin strands of glass

**glass reinforced plastic (GRP)** type of material, called a composite, made from glass fibres embedded in plastic

**helm/helmsman** the helm is the equipment used to steer a boat. The person who controls the helm is called the helmsman.

**horsepower (hp)** a unit of measurement of the power of an engine equal to the work done by one horse, or 746 watts of electrical power

**hydrofoil** type of boat that rises up out of the water on underwater foils as it speeds up

**hydroplane** type of racing boat designed to skim across the water's surface. Only its two floats (called sponsons) and its propeller dip into the water. Keeping the main part of its hull out of the water reduces drag and makes the boat faster.

**inboard** inside a boat's hull. An inboard engine sits inside a boat's hull.

**inflatable** capable of being filled with air. An inflatable boat is made from rubber or plastic filled with air.

**knot** unit of measurement that is the same as a nautical mile per hour. (1 nautical mile equals 1.15 land miles or 1.85 kilometres.)

**lift** a force that acts upwards. A hydrofoil boat's underwater foils create lift as they cut through the water.

**monohull** a type of boat with one hull

**outboard** outside a boat's hull. An outboard engine is attached to the outside of a boat's hull.

**outrigger**  a frame or structure that holds a float out to one side of a boat

**performance**  a vehicle's speed, acceleration, stability and so on

**personal watercraft**  small motorbike-like vehicles designed for having fun close to shore

**plane**  a plane is a flat surface. The rear part of a power boat's hull is flatter than the bow and designed to skim over the water's surface. This is described as planing.

**planing hull**  type of hull that is designed to rise up on the top of the water when the boat is travelling fast. Planing hulls are usually flattened underneath so that they can skim the water's surface. Planing reduces drag and lets the boat go faster.

**propeller**  part of a boat that spins and pushes the boat through the water

**propulsion**  pushing, or propelling, a boat through water

**rudder**  a part of a boat that is swivelled underwater to steer the boat. Water hitting the angled rudder pushes the stern (back end) of the boat to one side and swings its bow (front end) round to point in a new direction.

**stepped (hull)**  a type of planing hull divided into two or more sections with a step between them. Stepped hulls reduce drag and let a boat go faster.

**streamlined**  designed to move through air or water easily, producing very little air resistance or drag. Smooth, gently curving shapes are more streamlined than rough or boxy shapes.

**throttle**  the part of an engine that controls the amount of fuel supplied to the engine. Opening the throttle lets more fuel into the engine, which speeds up. A powerboat's throttle is controlled by a lever in the cockpit.

**thrust**  a force that pushes a boat through the water. Thrust can be produced by a boat's propeller, a jet of water or a jet of gas from a gas turbine (jet) engine.

**transmission**  the gears and shafts that link a boat's engine to its propeller

**ultrasonic**  waves like sound waves but so high that they can't be heard by humans

**V12**  a type of engine with 12 cylinders, in two rows of six set at an angle to each other, forming a V-shape

**wake**  the waves that spread out behind a boat as it moves through water. The wake is caused by the boat's hull and propeller(s) churning up the water.

**wake-boarders**  people who skim across the water behind a boat, while standing on a board like a very short surf-board

**water-jet engine**  type of engine that propels a boat by pumping a high-speed jet of water out of the back of the boat. The pump is often driven by a jet engine.

# INDEX